A Reason To Sing

Devotions
by Mennonite Students

Edited and Illustrated
by Terry Stutzman

Library of Congress Number 83-80936
International Standard Book Number 0-87303-083-4
Printed in the United States of America
Copyright © 1983 by Faith and Life Press, 718 Main Street, Newton, Kansas

Unless otherwise indicated biblical quotations are taken from the Revised Standard Version of the Bible, copyrighted 1946, 1952, 1971, 1973 by the Division of Christian Education of the National Council of the Churches of Christ in the U.S.A. and used by permission of the publishers.

Foreword

During my undergraduate student days at Bethel College and Kansas State University, a small group of students and I often met to express our prayers and devotional meditations to God. At times my "quiet time" was intensely personal, reflecting the insecurities, the aspirations, and the doubts of my growing faith and self-understanding. On another day "our time together" was intentionally corporate, mirroring the deep sense of community, love, and support we felt for each other. Often we were passionately political, identifying with the agonizing hurts of the have-nots, the troubled, and also with the powerful in society.

Today's students also search, pray for, experience, and celebrate *a reason to sing* the Lord's song in their academic communities. This collection of thirty-four student-written devotions is offered to congregations and students by the Commission on Education as a resource for strengthening the devotional life of students and young adults. Let it be both an inspiration and an example for our "sharing with the Lord."

I would like to express my thanks to Terry Stutzman who has solicited, edited, and illustrated these devotionals. Students in Mennonite as well as other schools were asked to contribute their thoughts.

A Reason to Sing reflects a diversity of theological, cultural, and academic experiences. Its beauty is in this variety—young adults searching for and discovering a personal experience with God.

I would also like to express my gratitude to parents and to congregations for providing this resource as an encouragement for their students' devotional pilgrimages.

James L. Dunn
Secretary for Young Adult and Church School Education
Commission on Education

Newton, Kansas
March 12, 1983

Preface

I'd like to think it is basic optimism that makes me excited about planning things. I get an idea in my head, start visualizing the final product and can't quit thinking about it until I hold the new creation in my hands.

The day I found out about the devotional book, I was six weeks into my senior year at Bluffton College. Jim Dunn was on campus for a conference and joined me at lunch. When he told me about a project that he and his friends in the Department of Higher Education (DHE) had dreamed up, a devotional book written by and for Mennonite college students, I immediately tried to picture the end product. Such a book could be personal at the same time it presented a wide variety of students' experiences, I thought. And others' questions might help me sort through a few of my own, as well. Yes, depending on how this committee priced the book, I thought I would probably buy one.

Two months later, the project was mine to develop—to gather entries for, edit, and illustrate. I had no idea how to organize the next fourteen months of such responsibility, but I was excited. I felt fortunate to have Jim's encouragement, the support of the DHE, and experienced counsel from Elaine Sommers Rich, a writer and DHE member who was conveniently based in Bluffton. Each step I took in planning was as unfamiliar as the ones before it. But I always received positive responses—so many students, pastors, Student and Young Adult Contact Persons and missionaries had a part in encouraging writers and backing me up with their thoughts and prayers.

About ten months into the project, on one of those quiet Sunday afternoons while I was planning the illustrations, I began to wonder what title could encompass so many different feelings, perspectives, and approaches to faith and understanding. God's unending acceptance of our failures is the center of these devotions. We refer to the example of Christ again and again as the source of our understanding and our way to get beyond daily frustrations to contemplate that which is much more lasting. Our combined efforts at finding—and communicating—the love that works in any situation is what gives us energy. The light gets brighter bit by bit as we understand it more. For every chance we take in school, with friends, strangers, family, and with ourselves, Christ brings renewal at the end of our efforts. He is forever patient with us in our search for his peace. That is our reason to sing.

Terry Stutzman

Goshen, Indiana
February 1983

Contents

1. Living Quietly

Be still, and know that I am God.
Psalm 46:10

Paul tells the Thessalonians to "live quietly" (1 Thess. 4:11). What does it mean to "live quietly" in a university setting? The concept seems alien, incongruous with the constant feverish pace going on around us. Our existence is frantic, nonstop. We *must* get a paper done on time, or a homework assignment is due, or "only one hour to take this test?" My own life as a graduate student seems to consist of hurriedly trying to finish tasks. I don't usually walk for leisure, but to go somewhere to accomplish something in the outer reaches of the campus. What can we do to avoid getting breathlessly involved in our studies?

Paul exhorted the Thessalonians, who were apparently too busy, to "live quietly." The psalmist David stated God's concern for us in strong command form: "Be still, and know that I am God." When we get lost in the forest, we are to stop discerning the trees all around us and find a still, cool spot in the forest to commune with the Lord.

We need to set aside a little time each day to be alone with God. After all we are his creatures, and because of the way our souls are made, we need a close relationship with our Creator. Before beginning his ministry on earth, Jesus spent forty days in the wilderness getting to know his Father; we need to know him better as well.

Dear Lord, please help me to slow down to think of you more often, to worship with you privately. Thank you for the everyday tasks you have given me. Guide me into thinking of them as service to others and subsidiary to the strengthening and nurturing of our relationship. In Jesus' name, Amen.

Robin Shealy is in his graduate studies in mathematics at the University of Illinois in Urbana, Illinois.

2. Every Prayer Is a Prayer for the Spirit

The Lord's Prayer in Luke 11:2-4 is a little different than Matthew's version. It reminds me of a backpacking pilgrim, carrying around in the back pocket a checklist for the essentials of prayer: "Father. Thy name be hallowed. Thy kingdom come. Keep on giving us bread. Forgive us our sins. Lead us not into the test." This prayer is embedded in Jesus' teaching on prayer and it ends with these words: "...how much more will the Heavenly Father give the Holy Spirit to those who ask him!"

The Holy Spirit? How does the Holy Spirit fit into the Lord's Prayer? Here in Luke, we find the teaching on prayer, the Lord's Prayer, bound together with the promise of the Holy Spirit, as if to say the basis for all petition, for all asking, seeking and knocking is the Holy Spirit. That is what we are really asking for when we pray—the presence of the Spirit. And that is what we receive and what we find as the answer to our prayers—the presence of God in our daily lives.

Some may say this interpretation spiritualizes the petitions of the Lord's Prayer, which are actually about very concrete things: the coming of God's kingdom, the need for food, the nitty-gritty of human relationships, the reality of struggle in our lives. This teaching of prayer spiritualizes life's concrete realities while making the Spirit concrete for us.

So the request is for the hallowing of God's name. And the answer is the presence of the Spirit as the active agent through Jesus' followers, enabling them to witness to the glory of God (Acts 1:8).

The request is for the coming of the kingdom. And the answer is the Holy Spirit, whose presence is a sign for the preaching of good news to the poor, release to the captives, sight to the blind, liberty for the oppressed—the acceptable year of the Lord (Luke 4:19).

The request is for daily bread. And the answer is not just the assurance that hunger will be satisfied. The answer becomes the presence of the Spirit in the fellowship of our eating together.

The request is for the forgiveness of sins. And the answer again is the presence of the Holy Spirit, right there in the middle of all human interaction and disagreements—the Spirit working to challenge, to heal, to reconcile.

The request is not to be led into the test. And the answer again is the promise of the presence of the Spirit, teaching us in the very hour of trial what it is we are to say (Luke 12:11, 12).

The asking may be for many things, but the answer is always the presence of the Spirit in some concrete form. Every prayer is a prayer for the Spirit! And every answer to prayer is, at its core, the promise of the presence of God in our lives!

Lord, open our eyes to see that in all our asking and seeking, it is for your presence in our lives that we are looking. Open our hearts to your promise, that where we work for your kingdom, break bread together, forgive each other, and stand firm for your name, there will the Holy Spirit be in the midst of our lives. Amen.

Patricia Shelly is in a doctoral studies program in biblical interpretation at the Iliff School of Theology in Denver, Colorado.

3. Being Ashamed of Your Faith

For whoever is ashamed of me and of my words, of him will the Son of man be ashamed when he comes in his glory and the glory of the Father and of the holy angels.
Luke 9:26

I tried to appear casual as I walked into the third floor classroom and took a front row seat. After 2½ years at a small Christian college, I was attending my first class at a huge, inner city university.

The course was Magazine Article Writing. The professor, a sixty-three-year-old man dressed entirely in black, lost no time informing us that his policy was open criticism of all articles in class. He spent the first class period telling horror stories of former students he had intimidated—students whose fear had turned them into top-rate writers. The man obviously had no mercy.

As the semester progressed, I sensed in him a deep bitterness and mocking attitude toward Christianity. His lectures were often interspersed with barbs about Christians whose "prayers" for someone's conversion were little more than emotional blackmail. His opinion of Christians was that all were either scheming hypocrites or weak persons who used God as a crutch.

I became determined to show him that not all Christians were closed-minded or unintelligent. I would break his stereotypes by writing thoughtful, well-articulated articles that would gain his respect.

The second article I wrote was on private Christian education. After thoroughly researching the subject and interviewing the vice-principal of the Mennonite high school I had graduated from, I began compiling the article.

I had intended to present the pros and cons of Christian education in an unbiased way. However, in my eagerness to appear open-minded, I went overboard. I sidestepped fairness and began to focus critically on what I saw as the legalism and narrowness of fundamentalist Christian education. It wasn't that I distorted the facts about Christian education—I simply didn't tell the whole story. I never really talked about all the nonfundamentalist Christian schools, like the one from which I had graduated, whose policies I *did* agree with. As the article neared completion, I became aware of what was happening, but I was too fearful of my teacher's criticism to slant the story more positively.

The article came back with glowing remarks, but the feeling of accomplishment was hollow. I knew I had simply told him what he already believed about Christian education. In trying to please him I had compromised myself. I knew Christ was disappointed in me.

The article sits in a drawer now. I didn't show it to anyone but my parents. I don't think I'll throw it away—it's too powerful a reminder of Christ's warning in Luke 9:26. If we're ashamed of him and his words, he'll be ashamed of us.

Ann Martin is a 1983 graduate of Messiah College in Grantham, Pennsylvania. She majored in communications and minored in English.

4. God Is Our Refuge

Psalm 46

Dear God,

I hate this day! I feel as if I am at the bottom of a hole. There is a rope just above my head waiting to be grasped, but chunks of dirt and rock keep falling toward me and blocking my view. Get me out of here!

There are so many things to be done all at once, but I can only do one thing at a time. How much do the profs expect, anyway? I suppose it is my fault for not starting some of this sooner, and I really didn't have to say yes when I was asked to do the decorations for the banquet, but it still isn't fair! I can't handle this.

How can you say, "Quit worrying about it"? Don't you see that I have to get all of these things done I promised? I don't want to do a lousy job of them, either, but there's simply not enough time.

I'm having a rotten day and I shouldn't be. Look outside—beautiful blue sky, clouds sailing overhead, but there might be a snowstorm for all that I notice it. There are so many friendly people around, but I'm so preoccupied with worrying that I can't even enjoy their company. How miserable I am!

Wait a minute there. "Slow down," is that what you're saying? Maybe, but it seems to me that I should be speeding up, or I'll never get things out of the way by the weekend. . . .

I think I hear what you're saying. I'm so full of worries that I'm not even taking time to talk to you. I'm trying so hard to get through on my own that I'm ignoring the help you're offering me. Why didn't I see that before?

All right, I accept. What have I got to lose? The work won't go away, I know, but it doesn't seem so terrible anymore. With your help I can work through everything a little at a time, without losing any sleep over it. I can take time and talk to people, too, instead of ignoring everything but my own problems. Much better! God, thank you for helping me to see this. Help me to remember it the next time a day like this comes along.

Your loving daughter,

Jo

Joanne Epp is a second-year music student at Swift Current Bible Institute in Swift Current, Saskatchewan.

5. The Final, Final Exam

Matthew 7:21-23

Matthew 7:21-23 is one of the most shocking and sobering passages in all the Bible. It is shocking because those who have prophesied, exorcised demons, and performed many miracles for the cause of Christ think their place in heaven is well assured. But Jesus solemnly declares that they were never known by him and that they did evil (literally: *lawlessness*) rather than good. As in Matthew 25:41 they are banished into eternal punishment. Irony abounds in that they who claimed intimacy with Jesus are told they are unknown by him; they who prophesied are prophesied against; and they who cast out evil spirits are themselves cast out as evil. This passage is sobering because it is a call to self-examination. We must ask ourselves if this could ever happen to us.

A first response to this passage might be: "Yes, that's shocking and a tragedy, but that could never happen to me!" The passage may not seem very real to us because we have a hard time relating to exorcisms and miracles. Perhaps its true meaning may be brought out more clearly to a modern Anabaptist Mennonite by the following paraphrase of verse 22: "Lord, Lord, as your community, did we not raise a prophetic voice against war and social injustice, as your community did we not cast out the MX missile and the B-1 bomber, as your community did we not do many good works through VS, MDS, and MCC?" Will these wonderful works assure us a place in heaven?

The final, final exam for entrance into the kingdom of heaven is not whether one does lip service to Jesus as Lord or even does wonderful works, but whether one does God's will. But what is the will of God when even miracles done in Jesus' name are not enough?

A very large part of God's will for us is obedience. Any good Mennonite already knows that, and scores of Mennonite good works are readily apparent. But Matthew's lawless ones had their works, too—works far more impressive than ours.

The second crucial component of doing God's will is love and self-surrender to God. Ostensibly working for God, yet not accomplishing God's will means taking pride in the miracles God works through oneself, glorifying oneself rather than God, ministering to others but with ulterior motives, being zealous but hypocritical.

During my senior year at the University of Kansas I was planning to enter seminary and become a pastor. I was studying New Testament Greek, religion, and church history. I was the president of an Inter-Varsity Christian Fellowship chapter, and was supervising IVCF's small fellowship/Bible study/discipleship groups on campus. People observing me might have thought, "Oh, what a good Christian he is" (at least I thought so myself). But when my life and activities that year began to fall to pieces, I eventually realized what a hypocrite I was. I was interested in self-glory, not in God's glory. Though I prayed for guidance, I did what I wanted and used God as a cosmic rubber stamp for my activities. Though I did many activities in Christ's name, I was not really doing *God's* will, but my own.

To pass our final, final exam let us continually examine ourselves—our motivations, our desires, our love. Let us ask if Matthew 7:21-23 does not in at least some small way apply to us. Let us examine ourselves, lest we hear on that day: "I never knew you; depart from me, you evildoers."

Mark D. Stucky is a 1983 graduate of the Associated Mennonite Biblical Seminaries in Elkhart, Indiana. He has a master of divinity in pastoral ministry.

6. Character Building

Romans 5:1-8

Isn't it strange how personal struggles often hold hidden blessings for the growing Christian?

During my first semester of Bible school, I was slowly becoming acquainted with other students, but was often content to be by myself as I integrated into my new surroundings. Just as I was independent of home and family, I wanted to be independent at school.

It was after accidentally breaking my wrist that I realized the potential for growth found in being dependent upon someone. I needed help to get dressed, to wash, and to eat. In asking for assistance, I was showing my vulnerability, letting down my defenses, and allowing people to know me. From others who thoughtfully volunteered to help, I discovered love and kindness.

What initially had been a painful experience ultimately turned my heart and thoughts to praise, patience, and thankfulness for the development of myself and the hope my classmates offered through Christ's love. A person needs fellow Christians and should not neglect to ask them for help.

Paul's letter to the Romans articulates my own experience of Christian growth through the sequence of "suffering that produces perseverance; perseverance, character; and character, hope." In our powerlessness, God indeed demonstrates his love for us.

Ruth Preston is a second-year biblical studies student at Swift Current Bible Institute in Swift Current, Saskatchewan.

7. Open-book Tests

And as he sat at table in the house, behold, many tax collectors and sinners came and sat down with Jesus and his disciples. And when the Pharisees saw this, they said to his disciples, "Why does your teacher eat with tax collectors and sinners?"
Matthew 9:10, 11

It seems to me that Jesus' life was the text for an open-book test. Anytime someone asked anything of him, the answers were there. For three years people were prying into Jesus' life with questions: What? How? Why? Why? Why?

The Gospels offer a record of some of those times of questioning, but what about the other times? What kinds of questions did the tax collectors and sinners have? Maybe they weren't interested in the questions of the scribes and Pharisees. Maybe the last things they wanted were more religious rules and regulations. But they did want a friend, someone to sit down and eat supper with them and someone who would listen to them. Here again, Jesus was that open textbook. He let others see him—who he really was inside. He didn't pretend to be anything else, no matter where he was or who he was with.

Now that's a challenge to me! Do I really let people see who I am, including the spiritual side of me? Do I "change my tune" depending upon the situation at hand, hoping to avoid conflict?

Jesus spent a lot of time with people who were not following his way. I'm sure their conversations dealt with a wide variety of topics. I spend time with non-Christians too, especially on a university campus. I have non-Christian friends here, and we also talk about a wide variety of things, but am I as open and as honest as Jesus was?

My life and your lives are open textbooks too. We may be the only text to Christ and Christianity that our friends have. The temptation is to close the book occasionally, not to tell our true thoughts and the real reasons for our actions, even when friends are asking questions. The spiritual side of us is a hard chapter to have open sometimes, but it may be the most important one.

We need to be continually asking for God's leading as we spend time with those who are not Christians. People are often questioning within themselves, if not verbally. It's a bit scary to think of ourselves as one of their resources, but we are.

So I leave you with this challenge: be an open textbook to those around you as Jesus was to the tax collectors and sinners.

Jane Birky is a 1983 graduate of the University of Illinois in Urbana, Illinois. She majored in food and nutrition.

8. I Am with You Always

One experience each of us must face, whether college-bound or not, is growing up and leaving the protective arms of home. Many articles are written for parents on how to cope with empty feelings when their children test their wings and leave the nest, but few mention the feelings of insecurity the young adult faces as he or she enters the world alone.

The summer before my first year of college, feelings of doubt and uncertainty began to surface. I suddenly realized that when Labor Day rolled around I wouldn't be walking up the familiar sidewalk, entering the familiar high school building, and greeting familiar faces of lifelong friends. I knew the sidewalks would be different, the buildings large and foreboding, and friends few and far between. The life I had known for eighteen years would soon drastically change. I knew I would be far away from the home I loved so much when I needed security and love. I was scared. I had completely forgotten Paul's familiar words in Romans, ". . . nothing will ever be able to separate us from the love of God . . ." (Rom. 8:38, 39, LB).

Needless to say, when I entered college these feelings didn't miraculously go away. I wasn't immediately filled with happiness and a sense of belonging. As much as I had dreamed of college, I would have been the happiest girl in the world if I could have loaded every one of my worldly possessions back into our van, turned around and headed home—where I belonged! This general feeling continued through half of my freshman year. I was quite homesick and spent most of my time thinking about home and wishing I was there with Mom and Dad instead of at school by myself.

Since my first year of college I have learned a lot about coping with fear and loneliness. The direct advice given by David in Psalm 45:10, "I advise you, O daughter, not to fret about your parents in your homeland far away," (LB) caught my eye. Though I had read psalms many time before, this verse really held meaning for me that first year of school. It suddenly became clear to me that worrying about home and family members is not necessary because God is watching over us while we are apart from each other.

No matter how alone and afraid we feel, we are never truly alone. It is so easy when we are feeling lonely to fall into the trap of self-pity and forget that God is always there to lean on. Just before his return to heaven Jesus assured his disciples that he would be with them always. I believe that we too can be confident of his constant presence. If we truly believe the promise given in Matthew 28:20, "I am with you always, even to the end of the world," (LB) we need not fear even when faced with the most difficult situations—for we know our Lord is always with us.

Arnita Yoder is a senior mathematics education major at Bluffton College in Bluffon, Ohio.

9. The Word Becoming

My mailbox contained a letter from a college friend this morning. He reminded me that Jesus is the Word become Flesh. Because we live on this side of Easter, we have the tendency to remove the Flesh from the Word. Jesus' first disciples learned to know him first as man, *then* as God. They found it difficult to accept Jesus, the man, as God. We have the opposite difficulty. To prevent a "Sunday-school-answer" type of religion, it is necessary to have Flesh on the Word.

Some words lose their flesh because we use them with our minds in neutral. Of the many names given to Jesus, one of our favorites is *Lord*. Unfortunately, we often use this word unthinkingly because it sounds nice. When the first disciples acknowledged Jesus as Lord, it meant, "I am your servant" (and *servant* meant servant!). It meant that he was their personal Lord! It said, "Thy will be done." It showed loyalty and committed obedience.

Joy is another fine word. Many sermons make reference to it. It is an excellent word for songs, almost as popular as *love*. Unfortunately, the faces of too many choirs and congregations don't radiate the joy they sing about. Sermons ending with, "let's all be joyful," lack impact. Somewhere in our efforts to take God seriously we have taken *ourselves* too seriously. As a result Jesus has become a glum-faced Someone who never blinks on ninety-minute TV specials.

If Jesus never chuckled, grinned, or belly laughed (although sometimes he may have had a glint in his eye), why were the children attracted to him? Why is the New Testament filled with references to joy? On the contrary, Jesus himself offers us *complete* joy. Jesus must have had a good sense of humor. Most holy people do. For us to really know joy, Jesus needs to become a friend whose company we can enjoy.

Hope, *faith*, *grace*, especially *believe*—many words are meaningless without flesh. That's why Jesus came—to be the flesh that bridges humanity and God. Perhaps as we learn to know Jesus more from the other side of Easter, the Word will become more fruitful in our lives.

Bruno Dyck has junior standing as a business administration major at the University of Manitoba in Winnipeg. Currently in voluntary service in Strasbourg, France, he works on organizing the 1984 Mennonite World Conference.

17

10. Another Down Day

Hear my prayer, O Lord; let my cry come to thee! Do not hide thy face from me in the day of my distress! Incline thy ear to me; answer me speedily in the day when I call!
Psalm 102: 1,2

Dear Journal:

It's been another "down" day and I can't begin to see the light. Sometimes I wish that I could experience my life without having to depend on "good" days to get me through the rest. Depression seems so unproductive, especially when I'm supposed to be studying and writing term papers. I know that depression isn't new in this world by any means, nor is it for me, but sometimes I can't make any sense out of it.

On days like today, I don't appreciate persons trying to cheer me up by telling me to "Smile!"; a smile on the outside doesn't make the inside right. When I'm down, I need time to make myself come out of it, but sometimes my friends don't understand that, and that can make me even more depressed. What I would really like them to do is appear as if nothing is really wrong (I'm sure that they sometimes get depressed too!), or take the time to ask me if they can help. I may or may not tell them exactly what is bothering me, but I do appreciate an effort to show concern.

Yet, I think that I've learned a great deal about myself through my times of feeling down, even if my school work did suffer during those times. When I'm down, I spend a great deal of time thinking—time that is not wasted in my opinion. I've analyzed myself and my relationships to others and have come to some conclusions and insights that I might not have if I had been in an acceptable, "normal" state of mind. (For one thing, I've determined that a state of mind is quite relative, and to let society determine what is normal for me as an individual does not necessarily help me grow as a person.)

I think that I've gained objectivity with depressions; I've learned not to judge myself and others by the mood or state of mind that I am in presently, rather consider the situation carefully. Also, I hope that I am learning to accept fluctuations and cycles in my character. I always have been, and will probably always be, to some extent, an up-and-down kind of person instead of one of these stable-and-never-get-flustered types that I so admire but can't emulate.

So what I seem to be concluding is that a day like today which was definitely "down" is as much a part of me as my crooked teeth or dark hair. Hopefully, I can learn much more about myself and how I can relate to others with both "bad" and "good" days.

Thanks, journal, for listening. You've made me feel much better already.

Brenda Suderman is a 1983 graduate of Canadian Mennonite Bible College in Winnipeg, Manitoba. She majored in theology.

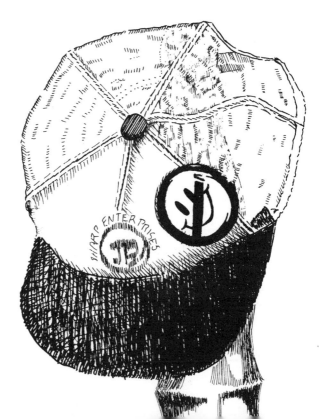

11. Bite the Bait

I will give you everything that
your Savior will not—
> The exotic, the alluring,
> The exorbitant, the daring...
>> if you will follow me.

And if you are a trusting disciple
I shall give you the master-prize.
(Oh, how I love your bulging eyes)

But first:

I will give you freedom from oppression—
> Psychedelic trips that no travel agency
> could ever fashion,
> Dope to help you cope,
> Beer to cure your fear,
> And colorful dreams from way back when
> will flash again and again.

Follow me and you will see what I
say come true.
Follow me and my supreme gift will
be given unto you.

But first:

I will give you freedom of expression—
Loose sex with whomever you desire
whenever you feel the passion.
I will give you poetic licentiousness
in all you write and sing.

I will give you everything:
All the world's desires;
And if you are a good disciple
delighting in what your bulging eyes do see

My master-prize I will *gladly* give to thee.

I bequeath unto you...Death.

O, God, I'm tired of the vices of this world. They are everywhere. And, even though I'm a Christian, I am still susceptible to these omnipresent temptations. Being "in the world but not of the world" is hard to achieve. In this world of "try it, you'll like it" crazes, it's all too easy to become swamped and to sink into the devil's mire.

In Apostle Paul's epistle to the Philippians (4:8), Paul gives directions on how to overcome the world's iniquities: "Finally, brethren, whatever is true, whatever is honorable, whatever is just, whatever is pure, whatever is lovely, whatever is gracious, if there is any excellence, if there is anything worthy of praise, think about these things." We do not need Satan's ephemeral "pleasures" when we can have Jesus' eternal satisfaction.

Christine Troyer is a 1983 graduate of Bluffton College in Bluffton, Ohio. She majored in biology.

12. Smoke in My Eyes

Matthew 12:14-21

It didn't take me long to classify Alice Smith a cynic. Alice disliked John Bunyan, John Milton, and Jerry Falwell with mounting disdain. More than once I sat in class, my eyes glued to my desk, while she ranted and raved. Any response on my part would have only fueled the fires—both mine and hers.

Academically she was excellent. She demanded much and put her whole self into getting the best from us as her students. My first semester with her was almost over when she returned an ungraded paper to me. By requiring a rewrite, she prodded me to new literary heights.

It was near the end of the next semester that my understanding of Alice included some of her personal struggles as well as academic standards. She nominated me for an honorary speech competition and coached me in my preparation.

One day after answering my questions about the speech, she talked further. She told me about her struggle for faith, her divorce from her deacon husband, and her agony over her infant grandson's cancer. She talked about needing friends to cry with her, and of wanting to believe.

I left that encounter still concerned about Alice's faith, but I wasn't so judgmental anymore. I saw that she wasn't trying to strip my faith; she was trying to build hers. Her anger was not at me personally, but festered from her own deep hurts. Then I tried to see Jesus meeting Alice.

I recalled Matthew's record of Jesus' way to deal with hurting people. Using a quote from Isaiah, Matthew reported that "a smoldering wick he will not snuff out" (Matt. 12:20, NIV). Smoldering wicks represent hurting, wounded people.

Wicks are made to burn brightly and give light. When one smolders instead of burning, it produces only irritating smoke. A dead wick or cinder is easier to live with than one that is constantly smoking.

Alice did produce smoke at times. Yet, when I see Jesus meeting Alice, I see him reaching beyond the smoke and seeing a little spark trying to burn. The spark means the wick isn't dead. I pray that with the tenderness so characteristic of his touch, he'll gently fan that spark to flame.

Nate Yoder is a senior history, English, secondary education major at Western Kentucky University in Bowling Green, Kentucky.

13. Looking into an Aquarium

My first aquarium consisted only of a small glass jar in which I kept vallisneria and two goldfish.

Life in the little aquarium was peaceful but a bit lonely for the fish. "It isn't good for the two to be alone," I said to myself. "I will make a better home for them with more companions and furniture to suit their needs."

I bought a metal-frame aquarium to replace that simple jar. I laid gravel and in it formed hills and put in a variety of plants; I installed a filter, an air pump, light, a thermometer, and a thermostatic heating unit to enhance the environment. I provided dietary fish food so as to spur growth. I also brought many new companions for the two beloved fish.

I was well pleased with what I had done and it was excellent in every way. I rejoiced whenever I thought of them in my leisure and they made my devotion to them a joy.

One day, while replenishing the water, I saw three little fish lying dead in a bundle of Cambomba behind a hill. Oh! What had happened? Postmortem lesions revealed that they had died of an attack by another species that wanted to extend its control of the ecosystem. The other fish's readiness and alertness for attack indicated that they were culprits of this first crime.

"Have I provided insufficient space and food for you, my dear friends?" I asked resentfully. "From the very first day, I have been attentively furnishing all your needs. You have fresh water from above and delicious foods with all tastes and nutrients. You don't have to care about the food remnants, for I remove them to prevent fouling your living place. What have I not done?

"Little fish, stop your arrogance and mourn for what you have done. Learn the way your caretakers show you their great mercy and love. It is not too late for you to do things decently and in order. If you don't you will be chastened and condemned the day your master becomes sick of you.

"Oh! Little fish, how I want you to know about the ethics for relating to your neighbors and masters! How should I tell you to make you understand?''

From that day onward, harmony left the aquarium. The fish were on watch in fear that they might not be safe while patrolling their own territory. They wanted to hurt each other physically because of their aggressive nature and their possessiveness. They needed to be separated.

Yesterday, because of my own greed for more advantages, I betrayed and hurt the feeling of my close friends. I felt proud of the craft I had invented, believing that I was the most cunning of all.

Later, when I looked at my aquarium closely, I pictured myself swimming repugnantly together with the fish. I waved my hand to them and they responded with their fins. I had a better understanding of them. Meanwhile, I had gained a new evaluation of my every deed.

Leung Wing—Kay (Peter) is a student at Chinese University in Kowloon, Hong Kong.

14. The Gift of Life

Take care to live in me, and let me live in you.
John 15:4 (LB)

In a gentle whisper, Christ comes to our hearts to say "Live in me. Come, *feel* the warmth in my forgiveness! *Explode* in the wonder of my love! *Grow* in my humility. *Touch* my soul and witness the courage needed to do God's will. *Stretch* your heart to grasp my pain and suffering on the cross. *Sense* the liberation in my resurrection, for now you can become all that God has given you the capacity to become! *Live in me*, like a free spirit fed by the strength in my truth.

"Now, I will come down to you, to your little world to *live within you*. I, Jesus, will be your hands that feed a naked, starving people. I will be your eyes which cry for the lost. I will be your mouth that speaks of a fresh, new life of promise. My spirit will spread into your mind, your heart and your soul. I will give you the inner desire to never stop growing. My love will make you *whole* again."

Let us go out beyond the walls and boundaries to share our precious life with the universe. Together, we will be strong and fearless, committing ourselves to God as his people. We will set free all the trapped and hurting souls. We will make the earth rejoice in our feelings of hope, trust, and freedom. *Celebrate*! We have the gift of life!

Esther Ruth Neufeld is a second-year theology student at Canadian Mennonite Bible College in Winnipeg, Manitoba.

15. Dealing with Rejection

1 Corinthians 13

If you've ever been rejected in love, you know how it hurts. Chances are you've played the martyr. The game is quite simple. All it requires in the way of talent is a small amount of masochism. Let me share four simple steps to help you succeed at this game.

Step one: Turn on sad music on your stereo and listen to all the other people who have been rejected in love. Read your old love letters and reminisce.

Step two: Ask God, "Why me? Of course I have had sterophonic, vista-vision fantasies, but God, I'm human. I did behave myself. I try to honor you. I've kept our appointments. Basically, I'm a good person."

Step three: Mope. Do nothing but lengthen your face and practice making a fat lower lip. This mask is conducive to pity and discourages any new relationships from developing.

Step four: Keep tabs on him or her. Decide if he or she has a new love. Once decided, look for this new love's strong points and tell yourself exactly what you're lacking. Sit in a lotus position and repeat these faults to yourself like a mantra. This is a great exercise for crushing self-esteem and fostering jealousy and bitterness.

Simple? It's a cinch. The problem is that by winning this game you become a loser. If you've tired of playing the martyr game, follow these four difficult steps to game-free living:

Step one: Read 1 Corinthians 13. Let it soak in. Reread it. Think about the Greek word *agape* which denotes God's love for you. Christ showed *agape* in asking God to forgive the very people that spit on him, mocked him, and crucified him. Thank God always for this love. Seek to know Christ better.

Step two: You say you're still in love? Love your former love with *agape. Agape* wants only the highest good for another. *Agape* "is very patient and kind, never jealous or envious, never boastful or proud, never haughty or selfish or rude. . . . It does not hold grudges." (LB) Whenever this person comes to mind, pray for him or her. Let go and put that person in God's hands. Pray for the fullness of Christ's joy and peace in his or her life. Grudges and bitterness cannot stand up to prayers like that.

Step three: Love your neighbor. There are people around you who are hurting. They need you. If you live in a dorm, make friends with the foreign student on your floor; bake brownies for your neighbor; make your "roomie's" bed. Tell people how much you appreciate them; take time to listen to others. Listen beyond their words to their hearts. This is a sure guard against self-pity.

Step four: Thank God for the plan God has for your life, and rededicate your life to God. This is the hardest step, but it is extremely important. It requires an act of the will.

In the garden Jesus cried, "My Father, if it be possible, let this cup pass from me: nevertheless not as I will, but as thou wilt" (Matt. 26:39). Jesus foresaw the trials and pain he would go through, but he didn't depend on his feelings. He submitted his will to God's. The feelings followed later.

If you have been rejected, you don't have to get depressed. Remember, "There are three things that remain—faith, hope, and love—and the greatest of these is love [*agape*]." (LB)

Benita Kornhaus is a 1983 graduate of Bluffton College in Bluffton, Ohio. She majored in English and social psychology education.

16. Turning in the Talents

Matthew 25:14-30

My mind is void of inspiration. For an entire week I've been wracking my brain, trying to think of an appropriate subject for a devotion. I've made the task more difficult by placing deadlines and other criteria on myself. It seems that I'm always doing this. I try too hard to do everything perfectly.

Let me give you an example. When I write a paper I struggle to phrase everything in exactly the right way. I'm not content to write, then rewrite. I have to write, scratch out, start over, write, rewrite, consult Webster and Roget, rewrite again, then finally type. But my perfectionist characteristics don't stop at the writing stage. They carry over into the typing as well. I can't remember how many papers I've typed twice because I can't tolerate my dumb little mistakes. Of course, not all of the tedium is for naught, as the satisfaction of a good grade is definitely a reward. However, I wonder how much less particular I could be and still do as well, and how much better a person to be around I could have been in the process.

Every time I catch myself doing something of this nature I ask myself, "Why am I such a perfectionist—to please myself or to please others?" I haven't found all of the answers yet. I know that part of the reason is that I am a proud person. I want things with my name attached to them to be done well. I want to feel a sense of accomplishment and, unfortunately, I want to know that others feel I've done well also.

God wants us to be satisfied with our work; however, working overtime to achieve the satisfaction of others certainly borders on unhealthy pride. Jesus categorized this kind of unhealthy pride (arrogance) with a long list of undesirable human characteristics (Mark 7:20-23).

In addition to being a matter of pride, my actions reflect the feeling that I've been given a number of talents which I need to use to their full potential. Jesus told the story of a man who entrusted his money to his servants while he went on a journey. The servant who was given five talents (a sum of money) brought back ten, and the servant who received two talents returned with four. Both men were praised for using their talents for their master. The servant who was given one talent was afraid of losing it. He buried his talent and returned to the master only what was given him in the beginning. Because he failed to use his talent, it was taken from him and given to the servant with ten talents.

This parable tells me that God expects us to use the gifts he has given us. Yet God doesn't expect us to abuse ourselves in trying to please him. Although it sometimes seems that others are demanding total perfection in more tasks than we can deliver, both we and they must recognize our humanness.

It's important to take on tasks that require the use of our talents. It's also important to take these tasks seriously and desire to do them well. But like everything else, too much of a good thing is no longer good. We all must learn to give a project our best shot, and then be content with our work knowing that God is satisfied with it also.

Lisa Janzen is a senior mathematics and speech communication major at Bethel College in North Newton, Kansas.

17. Where Is God?

Psalm 8 Psalm 14

God is in tree-coated mountains—mountains meeting in a cursive "V," with patches of dandelions mingling with smaller, dainty-white wild strawberry blooms. God is in tall, slender deciduous trees balancing like dancers on the mountains, their naked trunks forming silhouettes against the daylight. Nature has always spoken of God, but God does not need bright blue skies or two-toned grass blades to be.

God is in the soft-cheek kisses of brown-skinned women greeting each other on Sunday mornings in a tiny urban church. God is in the antics of great minds that create a skyscraper. God is in the tears of a lost child, somehow on the wrong Saturday morning train as she travels to see her godmother.

Late on a cold, tired afternoon, I boarded a crowded subway train. There was one space on the cold, smooth stainless steel benches for me to sit. As I settled wearily down, a woman, carrying a parcel, stepped onto my car. Then I noticed that the parcel was a baby wrapped in layer upon layer of fuzzy blankets. The woman planted her feet firmly on the littered floor, awkwardly clinging to her baby and the car's support pole.

God was in that woman with the parcel, and I knew it. I knew the baby was more than a shopping bag from Macy's or a book sack from the public library. The day was windy and the temperature had dropped below zero. No doubt the woman's arms were weary of handling her bulky child, but she knew the unspoken subway rule about seats: first come, first served.

I knew I needed to give my space on the cold metal to that woman. I knew the parcel was life and God was in life. But I did not rise. I focused my eyes on a spot on the floor where someone had ground a cigarette butt with a shoe until it burst. I ignored the woman. The train began to rock and jerk and roll again.

Sometimes it is easier to explain God in trees and birds and dainty flowers.

Mary Ann Zehr is a student at Goshen College, Goshen, Indiana. She spent a year in voluntary service in Bronx, New York.

18. Relaxing Spiritual Standards

Whoever then relaxes one of the least of these commandments and teaches men so, shall be called least in the kingdom of heaven; but he who does them and teaches them shall be called great in the kingdom of heaven. For I tell you, unless your righteousness exceeds that of the scribes and Pharisees, you will never enter the kingdom of heaven.
Matthew 5:19, 20

I remember an argument we had in my ninth grade civics class concerning the morality of the death penalty. The point was made about Jesus telling us to "turn the other cheek." The teacher, a Christian who favored the death penalty, said that people are only expected to "turn their cheeks so far." I remember feeling angered that this teacher, who claimed to believe in the Bible as the divinely inspired Word of God, could so easily bring down the words of Christ to comfortably fit within his own rationalizations. Instead of trying to use Christ's words as a higher standard of righteousness, he made them meet with his own lower human standards.

My civics teacher was not a bad man—just typical. It is easier to relax the standards God has set for us than to constantly struggle to bring ourselves up to what God wants us to be. It is easier to lie (Well, maybe I stretched the truth just a little), to cheat on our income tax (The government won't miss it), to talk about people behind their backs (I don't want to say anything bad about Louise, but), to buy that extra blouse or record album (I guess I really didn't need this, but I couldn't resist), to support militarism (I don't want war any more than you do, but we've got to defend ourselves). Unfortunately, the fact that these modes of behavior are easier does not give them any special virtue.

I am not saying that Christians can be perfect. We are human, after all. Being human, however, does not excuse us from *trying* to attain the spiritual perfection that Christ told us we were to have. It is difficult to tell the truth all the time, to choose honesty over personal gain, not to speak unkindly of others at times, to go without something we want, or to adopt views that are not popular with most of

33

society, and we will not always succeed in doing so. However, we can recognize that we are sinning when we relax these standards that God has set for us, and we can ask forgiveness for these sins instead of shrugging them off as "normal" human nature.

Of course, we are not to adopt a holier-than-thou attitude either; pride is as much a sin as anything else, and we cannot witness effectively to others if we consider ourselves a moral cut above them. If we can show instead that we are honestly aware of our human failings, and demonstrate that we are sincerely struggling to overcome these failings so that we might be more pleasing to God, then we might cause others to reevaluate the limitations of their own characters. We can show that as Christians, we know that God expects more of us than mere human nature.

Kathleen R. Kern is a 1983 graduate of Bluffton College in Bluffton, Ohio. She majored in English.

19. Mark's Trial: Day One

Stone.

The building was stone.

Imposing and tastefully impressive, it marked the center of Cleveland. "United States of America Federal Court" read the window, and just below it a smaller sign: "Fallout Shelter."

The curbs framing the city block were marble.

We cluttered the edifice with our banner:
> "Registration leads to the draft, leads to war, leads to death.
> Jesus said, 'Do not kill.'"

We littered the passing population with Mennonite propaganda:
> A letter from church leaders to Ronald Reagan on our behalf.
> People would accept our words if we could make even fleeting eye contact and exchange a smile.

> People going to and fro about their business just like you and me.
> Just like the Selective Service data processing team.
> Just like the director of compliance for Selective Service.
> Just like the Cleveland District Attorney.
> Just like Mark.

Ironic how we all came together.
> we all walk through the same door
> up the same marble stairs worn into little basins in the middle
> into the same courtroom
> chatter about the same weather.

Then as the gavel drops, snatch our scripts and prepare for the day's business:
> The United States of America vs. Mark Arden Schmucker.

The cocky bronze eagle spread above the bench in suspended flight defines our roles:
> "Order!" hiss the arrows in its right talons.
> "Integrity!" pleads the olive branch in its left.
> "Injustice!" screams my mind as the day of judgment begins.

We eye this religion's gods:
> twelve jurors, all with next of kin with military connections

none with moral objections to war
one taking a nap.

We eye Mr. Arbeznik, the prosecuting attorney.
We watch him stack the deck—within the rules
    determined to build an airtight argument:
        no reasonable reason exists to doubt Mark's guilt.
And we remember that only days before, Arbeznik had pleaded with
  his higher-ups to drop this case:
    "We should not be prosecuting this fellow!" he had said.
    But now it is the last day of the work week, and duty calls.
    Sadness fogs my glasses.

We hear, "Objection your Honor!"
    shouted whenever witness to Mark's faith and motives are ap-
    proached in a testimony.
The judge replies, "Sustained. Irrelevant."
And yet we endure hours of agonizing detail to prove:
    Mark Arden Schmucker did NOT register with Selective Service.
How the research clerk not only searched for:
    Mark Arden Schmucker, "S-C-H-M-U-C-K-E-R,"
    but "Mark ANDREW Schmucker," "Mark Arden SMUCKER,"
    All other young men with first name "MARK,"
    as well as FIRST name "Schmucker" (in case he had become
    confused and written his name in the wrong order).
I squirm with resentment.

In my more poetic moments, I become melodramatic.
    Mark, the sacrificial lamb.
    Victim of an upright conscience.
    Persecuted for taking "In God We Trust" off the silver and into
    the streets.
Guilty for *DOING*
nothing.
In the land of the free.

SO much at stake,
Yet even a five-year prison sentence would
    pale,
    blanch
        in the light of the servant—
            emptied

        humbled
        dying a stinking, humiliating death on a cross.
And the power of powerlessness drives home.

"He makes wars cease to the end of the earth;
    he breaks the bow, and shatters the spear,
    he burns the chariots with fire!
Be still, and know that I am God!" (Psalm 46:9, 10)

Ann Weber is a 1983 graduate of
Goshen College in Goshen, Indiana. She majored in music and
church ministries.

20. Experiencing the Presence of God

Psalm 23

At the edge of a lake on the second day of a canoe trip I waited, hoping the rain would soon stop. The overcast sky and constant drizzle gave the impression that it could rain for days. I studied the horizon for some time before spotting a small white cloud peeking over a hill far away. With eager anticipation I watched it slowly draw nearer and after half an hour it spread over two hills. Then I was sure that the sky would clear and that next day would bring clear weather.

Suddenly the thought struck me: This is how faith works! We get a small glimpse of revelation which points beyond itself to the mighty power of God, our Shepherd. Then we have confidence in the future.

When I read the Bible, especially the psalms, it becomes evident that these authors wrote from the perspective of a regular awareness and experience of God's presence. As a shepherd, David knew the trust which sheep put in their shepherd. He was able to put complete trust in God to meet his needs as well, because God, the great Shepherd, had promised to sustain. David could walk through the dark valleys without fearing the unknown because his loving Shepherd guided the way.

As Christians confronted with difficult choices and uncertain paths, it is essential that we learn to perceive God around us in our world and that we follow him. If, like uncooperative sheep, we try to go off on our own, we risk getting lost in a wilderness of confusion. Rather, we must recognize the Shepherd as he walks beside us in daily activities. We must trust in his leading.

The next morning as I paddled the canoe in the warm sunshine I was confident and thankful, for I knew my Shepherd was leading the way.

Jim Brown is in the Master of Divinity program at the Waterloo Lutheran Seminary in Waterloo, Ontario.

21. The Answer of the Tongue

The plans of the mind belong to man, but the answer of the tongue is from the Lord.
                    Proverbs 16:1

I was waiting for choir practice to begin when I heard about the death of my friend's father. The man had been sick for a long time, so his death was a release to him, and since I had never met him I couldn't feel the loss for myself. But I loved my friend. The choir director kindly let me cry while the rest of the group went on singing.

After rehearsal, I looked for my friend, not knowing what to say or do, but wanting to be with him. Someone had taken him to the bank; he was planning to fly home that same afternoon. When I finally found him in his room, his things were all packed and piled around him. He paced back and forth, pale and shaky and dry eyed, his pain nearly a physical presence and crushingly raw. It took an effort to enter the room.

We talked, but I don't remember the words. His visiting aunt, sister to his father, came in and graciously accepted my puny phrases of condolence. I felt myself to be horribly out of place. I had no right to be there, but I couldn't leave. My friend was hurt; I wanted to take the pain away. I recognized his father's death as necessary and beneficial in the long run, but sharing that would not have eased my friend's grief, so I said nothing. I had imagined that when I saw him we would cry together, but he was still too stunned for that. He seemed to be keeping an iron grip on his self-control, almost as an automatic reflex, until he could return home and begin to sort things out. He was so strong and so vulnerable. I saw no way to help him.

I left him with his aunt and returned to my room. Then I cried—for my friend's hurt, my own inadequacy, past griefs, and my friend's too-sudden departure. I was jealous that others friends had been able to do things for him and that I had been deprived of action on his behalf. I wanted to prove my friendship in some unforgettable way, but I had merely stood there, my hands hanging uselessly at my sides.

Then I cried at the realization of my selfishness, and I thanked God that I hadn't been able to carry out my plans.

That evening, another friend told me how much my visit was appreciated. Apparently it had been enough to sit and share grief silently. In spite of my blundering, God had been able to send some comfort through me to my friend.

Thank you, God, for making the profane sacred. Thank you for shaping my misbegotten efforts into your works of beauty and joy.

Lynne Carol Martin is a graduate student in English and Old Testament at the University of Manitoba and at Canadian Mennonite Bible College in Winnipeg.

22. When God Directs Our Lives

We know that in everything God works for good with those who love him, who are called according to his purpose.
Romans 8:28

When I finished high school, I felt led to study nursing. My family did not like the idea, for they wanted me to study a more "serious" career. I prayed for a long time, asking God to do his will in my life. He knew my vocation and aptitudes better than I did. I applied to a private university and was accepted in the School of Nursing.

What I really liked about the profession was the direct contact I had with the patients and the opportunity of talking to them about the love of God. When I knew I had been accepted, I thanked my Lord for allowing me to study what I had chosen, and for showing me his will.

As I advanced in my studies, I realized that nursing offers even more than I had wished. There are many ways to help people in their physical and mental health, and more importantly, to show the actions of God in different situations.

But something unexpected happened. The financial support from my father ceased and I could not attend the university any longer. I prayed, asking the Lord, "Why? Why could I not have a normal life so that I could finish my studies and begin working?" While reading the Bible, I found Romans 8:28 again, and thanked God for his promises and for the faith he was renewing in me.

Then, a new opportunity came. An uncle invited me to stay in his home so that I could attend a public university. I prayed again: "Lord, your will be done; if you want me to go, if it is for the good, then let everything happen." And it happened!

It is not easy to enter the public university because there are many applicants and the entrance exams are difficult. But I passed the exams and am now studying nursing in one of the best universities in Colombia. I was given credit for the three semesters I had already done, with the exception of two subjects. Even that helped me, for I know more now and am preparing myself to do a good job.

In the process, I got acquainted with the Mennonite Church in Bogota and became baptized there. I am also attending meetings with other university students who are interested in helping needy people.

So, I know by experience that "... in everything God works for good with those who love him."

Egda C. Quevedo is a junior nursing student at the Universidad Nacionale de Colombia in Bogota, Colombia, South America.

23. Who Is This Man Jesus?

Jesus and his disciples went on to the villages around Ceasarea Philippi. On the way he asked them, "Who do people say I am?"

They replied, "Some say John the Baptist; others say Elijah; and still others, one of the prophets."

"But what about you?" he asked. "Who do you say I am?"

Peter answered, "You are the Christ."
Mark 8:27-29 NIV

While walking on an old dirt road one day, a stranger decided to collect viewpoints on the perplexing question, "Who is this man Jesus?" As the stranger continued down the road he scanned the crowd for someone to answer this question.

A small child of seven bumped into the stranger and looked up smiling shyly in embarrassment. The stranger bent down and asked the child, "Who do you think Jesus is?"

The child wrinkled up his brow and then with calm assurance replied, "A big man with a long beard and a white robe, who sits in heaven and watches over me when I sleep."

Next the stranger saw a teenager deep in thought, walking slowly down the road. "Can you tell me who Jesus is?" he asked the girl.

The teenager replied, "Jesus is my strength in a very desolate hour. He is my help to solve problems. He is my friend and my comrade. With Jesus beside me I am never alone."

With a smile tugging at the corners of his mouth the stranger stood for a moment on the road. A young woman came trudging along the road carrying a small child. The stranger approached her and asked, "Who is this man Jesus?"

She answered, "He gave me this child to care for. Jesus gives me patience and kindness yet sternness with the child, even when the task seems almost impossible."

The last of the people the stranger confronted was an elderly man. "Who is this man Jesus?" the stranger asked.

"Jesus has been my everything throughout my entire life," the man replied, "and soon I shall meet my Lord in his home."

The stranger walked to the edge of the road and contemplated what he had been told that day, "A lot depends on me," he whispered softly.

The stranger in this prose represents Jesus, and the road he is traveling on represents each of our lives as we walk with Jesus day by day on our own spiritual pilgrimages. As each of us grows older, our knowledge of Christ and his importance to us becomes more advanced and in some respects clearer in our own minds.

Jesus is walking along the road talking to people of all ages. This idea portrays that Jesus will walk and talk to us if we are prepared to listen to what he has to say to us. We can't shut him out of our lives and expect him to reappear at the first sign of trouble. He'll walk with us through the valleys of darkness and over every mountain that seems too high for us to climb. Jesus will never forsake us.

Joanne Derksen is in the biblical studies program at Swift Current Bible Institute in Swift Current, Saskatchewan.

24. Living in Vital Union

And now just as you trusted Christ to save you, trust him, too, for each day's problems; live in vital union with him.
Colossians 2:6 (LB)

Satan never misses a chance to attack those who have been saved. He's always there, constantly watching to see us stumble and fall. If there is even the slightest hint of doubt, you can be sure that he's somewhere near.

My life seemed to be in order. My studies weren't too hard and my friends and I spent a lot of time pulling crazy college antics. But I had a feeling that I couldn't shake. It was like I was being followed by Satan and he was ready at any time for me to stumble. My friends did a good job of being there to get me over my depressions.

Then one night I had a dream: My friends and I were huddled in a circle, laughing and sharing life together.

I looked up and saw an evil spirit
laughing at me—
determined to get me.
I screamed and cried for help from my friends
but they couldn't see it.
The spirit kept coming
and in desperation I cried,
    "Lord, help me!"
And when I looked up again the spirit
was gone.

When I woke up, I remembered the dream as if it had really happened. Then I realized that even though my friends are always there, only Christ can save me. And he wants to. He just wants me to ask.

Lisa Yvonne Adams is a 1983 graduate of Bluffton College in Bluffton, Ohio. She majored in elementary education and kindergarten.

25. Sparks of Life

Matthew 5:13-16

"It only takes a spark to get a fire going." If we think of "fire," we can associate it with both positive and negative impressions. Fire provides warmth and pleasure for us and may also cook our food. However, fire raging through a forest or home or building may also bring much pain and suffering into life.

Like fire, our lives may also have both positive and negative implications. In Galatians 6:7, 8 we are told that a man reaps what he sows. One who sows to please the sinful nature will reap destruction, while one who sows to please the Spirit will reap eternal life from the Spirit.

Each day we are surrounded by many evil forces attempting to win our love and devotion. Living for Christ and sowing to please the Spirit put us into a spiritual battle. Praise God, for we do not have to fight it alone!

In the call to follow Christ and serve him we are commanded to be his witnesses and make disciples for him (Matt. 28:19, 20). Are we to preach from the podium or knock on doors on campus until the gospel has been heard by all? Why not be a servant and a friend? Everyone appreciates a gift, a visit, or a helping hand. It takes less effort to smile and extend a friendly greeting as you pass by than it does to frown.

Take time from your studies to invest your life in people. They will notice and appreciate your shining light—and may become inquisitive. What better way to share your special relationship with Jesus? Remember, God's children are the salt of the earth and the light of the world. What better time than now to spark the world with God's love and set it ablaze—before the evil sparks burn us out!

Irene M. Good is a 1983 graduate of the University of Western Ontario in London. She has bachelor of education and bachelor of applied science degrees.

26. Looking Past the Log

Why do you see the speck that is in your brother's eye, but do not notice the log that is in your own eye? Or how can you say to your brother, "Let me take the speck out of your eye," when there is the log in your own eye? You hypocrite, first take the log out of your own eye, and then you will see clearly to take the speck out of your brother's eye.

Matthew 7:3-5

I had a strong resentment against a fellow classmate last year. This guy came across as loudmouthed, insensitive, and narrow-minded. I wanted to punch him in the mouth every time he said something stupid in class. Gradually I realized that my dislike of him affected what I was learning in the course: I was so busy trying to control my temper (while at the same time nursing my resentment) that I wasn't hearing much of what the professor said.

I prayed that God would make my classmate more open to new ideas. I tried to convince myself that I had his best interests in mind when I asked God to change him. But nothing happened. He was still as big a jerk as ever.

One day, much to my displeasure, it dawned on me that I had no business praying for a change in him if I wasn't ready to pray for a change in myself. I skirted this issue for as long as I dared, but my growing discomfort was a sure sign that I had been given an instruction I wasn't following. Finally, to avoid being blatantly disobedient, I reluctantly approached God with my hot, sour pride and asked for a new attitude. It felt crummy to have to admit my own pharisaism but very soon I started to see more sparkle in the world.

A few days later I ran into my classmate in the library. He seemed to want to talk to me, which was very strange, since we'd hardly said more than half a dozen words to each other before. (It's odd how easy it is to dislike a stranger.) He told me some of his faith experiences, and I told him some of mine. We were amazed at how much we had in common. Toward the end of that conversation I told him I had been bothered by some statements he had made in class. He admitted being ashamed of having expressed some half-baked opinions, and he apologized, explaining that he had been working through some very confusing ideas, and that he had said some of those things to see whether people would challenge him.

Certainly he had some attitude problems of his own, but at least he was working on them. I, however, had been so concerned about his shortcomings that I never even considered the possibility of being at fault myself. The obnoxious person I wanted to punch in the mouth turned out to be surprisingly like myself.

Who changed more as the result of my prayer? It's difficult to know, and it probably isn't important. What matters is that the hard knot of enmity was loosened and finally dissolved because we each took responsibility for our parts in it.

Father, thank you for the gift of prayer.

Help us to use it wisely, remembering that honest confession is the basic ingredient.

Jesus taught that asking for your forgiveness means offering our forgiveness to others;

so too we know that responsibility for broken relationships lies within ourselves.

Help us to actively reconcile, instead of passively blaming, and deliver us from the sin of kidding ourselves.

Lynne Carol Martin is a graduate student in English and Old Testament at the University of Manitoba and at Canadian Mennonite Bible College in Winnipeg.

27. Spiritual Priorities

Matthew 19:13, 14

"What are you doing?" Jenny settled herself on a picnic bench and looked at me expectantly.

I looked up from my Bible. Her childishly chubby face was grubby and her nose desperately needed a good wipe.

"Just reading," I said, slightly irritated. I had planned on a nice, quiet devotional time here in the sun, but if Jenny was in the mood to chat it would certainly mess things up.

My annoyance was followed by a twinge of guilt. When the disciples had tried to prevent the little children from coming to Jesus, what had his reaction been? Did he thank them for keeping the little brats away so he could pursue more "spiritual" matters? Hardly. He criticized them for their stuffiness and welcomed the children with open arms (Matt. 19:13, 14).

Jesus certainly seemed to measure Christian effectiveness with a different yardstick than the one I use. I measure my effectiveness by the length of my devotions, the number of Scriptures I memorize, and the duration of my prayers. Christ seemed to care more about *being* than doing.

I am a chronic list-maker. My "Things To Do" list is always close at hand and gets updated constantly. The number of items I check off my list generally determines whether each day is a success or a failure.

There's nothing wrong with making lists—except when I carry this success-measured-by-accomplishment attitude into my spiritual life. Take devotions, for instance. Instead of viewing them as a time to put away life's pressures and distractions, I too often treat them as one more item to be checked off the list. The satisfied feeling I get when I complete my devotions can be remarkably similar to the feeling I get from doing my laundry or cleaning the bathroom—hardly the satisfied feeling of a well-nourished spirit.

So what's the point of all this? Only that I think Jesus would have put down the Bible and talked to Jenny, rather than retreating into the house so he could pursue spiritual maturity in peace.

Ann Martin is a 1983 graduate of Messiah College in Grantham, Pennsylvania. She majored in communications and minored in English.

28. Infirmity

Romans 8:35, 37

Though strength of body pass away
And scattered thoughts pervade my brains,
May best I serve you, Lord, I pray
With all the vigor that remains.

If miracle is not the plan,
Dramatic healing not your will,
Then let my narrow vision scan
The blessings gained from being ill.

Joel Miller is a 1983 graduate of
Bluffton College in Bluffton, Ohio.
He majored in chemistry and
biology.

29. Waiting

Lamentations 3:1-33

I hate to wait. I hate red stoplights, traffic jams, long lines. I hate watching precious minutes slip by. Often I've said: "*I can't wait* until this paper is done (or until I hear about that job application, until the end of the semester, until I get married. . .)." I am not alone. We live in an impatient, antiwait culture that invented microwave ovens, Concorde SSTs, credit cards, fast-food chains, and instant coffee.

However, in God's University named Life, waiting is a required course. We can choose to get angry when we have to wait, or we can learn to accept it. I, anyway, am a slow learner.

Waiting goes beyond petty annoyances. We wait as we search for a job in our ravaged economy. We wait as a loved one with a terminal disease slowly and painfully slips away. We wait as we pray that a strained relationship will heal and grow. As days drag into weeks and months, our angry impatience mutates into depression, bitterness, and fear. Happiness becomes a forgotten thing of the past. "Where is God as we wait? Why doesn't he do something? How can he let us down like this? How much longer will he let this go on?"

Lamentations speaks to a people in exile; a people who were in agony; a people who had seen their nation smashed; a people who experienced what had once been unthinkable horror; a people with hope that was dead. They were a people who had the choice either to curse God and become part of their victor's culture or to repent for their sins, seek God, and . . . wait.

The prophet Jeremiah knew agony. He expressed his feelings in this lament. He expressed how he felt about God—both the agony and the hope. Yes, it seemed that God had turned against them, but faith screams out over the roar of pain: God is loving, merciful, and faithful! "The Lord is good to those who wait for him, to the soul that seeks him. It is good that one should wait quietly for the salvation of the Lord" (vv. 25,26).

The Hebrew people waited in exile for seventy years before salvation came and they could return to their homeland. We may also have to wait a long time, a lifetime perhaps, until the Lord comes back. But in the meantime we must remember: "It is good that one should wait quietly for the salvation of the Lord" (Lam. 3:26).

Mark D. Stucky is a 1983 graduate of the Associated Mennonite Biblical Seminaries in Elkhart, Indiana. He has a master of divinity in pastoral ministry.

30. The Wisdom of the World

Where is the wise man? Where is the scribe? Where is the debater of this age? Has not God made foolish the wisdom of the world? For since, in the wisdom of God, the world did not know God through wisdom, it pleased God through the folly of what we preach to save those who believe. . . . For the foolishness of God is wiser than men, and the weakness of God is stronger than men.
1 Corinthians 1:20, 21, 25

I am a student at a state university. Academically, the competition for recognition is intense. After several encouraging classes, I found myself in the race—studying, testing, comparing, striving. Every day I would surround myself with university students, university professors, university ideas, and university goals. I listened to casual chatter about someone's convenient, no-fuss abortion; I chuckled at the atheistic professor's stabs at Christianity; and I wrote papers about religious folklore in literary works. Immersed in a world hostile to God, I was beginning to forget what it had been like to love God, to pray for his guidance, to believe in his sovereignty. I bought into the "me first" philosophy of worldly life.

Habitually, I kept up with the practice of Christianity. I went to church and Bible study. I passed out petitions for a nuclear freeze and with a conscious awareness of starving, third-world populations, I did not eat meat. My faith was buried in my social concerns and was not the source of them. Christianity was my religion—private, yet well organized, taking up only Sunday morning and Tuesday evening.

One Sunday, as I prepared to leave church with a list of the afternoon chores and activities neatly tucked in my Bible, I got news that a friend's sister had died. The finality of the announcement, the fresh pain, the exposed starkness of death stung me. I stood before my friend with my tidy religion and was jolted by the realization that the world and I had nothing to offer.

Looking at her, I saw peace, and hope, and grace, and mercy, and love. A triumphant, omnipotent, ominscient God stared back at me

with a steady, honest gaze. I embraced her and her faith and prayed
for the wisdom and mercy of God.

Renée Davern is a senior English
major at the University of Arizona
in Tucson.

31. On Blind Faith

Now faith is the assurance of things hoped for, the conviciton of things not seen.
                    Hebrews 11:1

Since I have become a graduate student in English, I have had to get a handle on modern secular thought and criticize literature from the perspective of a "modern thinker." When I consider the nature of my faith as a Christian, I remember something that occurred in the philosophy class I took during my freshman year in college. The particulars have faded into the past, but I recall that the class was discussing some philosophy that seemed clearly opposed to Christian thought. Another young man, grasping this philosophy as a well-thought position that supported his own disbelief, contrasted it with Christianity, venomously upholding the logic of the philosophy against the "blind faith" required for Christian belief.

I suspect that I had heard the phrase before, but I had never been exposed to such hatred of Christianity. Moreover, I had never seriously studied philosophies that reject Christianity. Since that time, especially in the last year, I have had the occasion to gain a greater understanding of different secular philosophies, and I must say that I have gained some sympathy for some of them. Although my faith has changed, I still believe.

Those who developed the great modern philosophies were committed to understanding the nature of life. Through observation and meditation often these people came to the conclusion that humanity creates its own institutions and social structures. In most cases this makes sense and Christians would not find it alarming. But when one considers that the church is an institution included in this hypothesis, and even God is considered a creation of humanity, Christians must begin to take exception to the idea. Aside from our earthly lives, they say, there is nothing.

If we take a moment to think about this idea, we will discover that we believe in God in different ways. The way our churches operate is certainly based on the way different congregations believe. We believe in a God we cannot see, so in varying degrees we choose the characteristics of the God we believe in based on the testimony of people of past ages as well as our own. But this does not mean that God is a human creation, a product of the fertile human mind. It only means that we cannot know with certainty that God exists.

This should not alarm us nor is it reason enough to lose faith, for as Hebrews 11:1 points out, faith is applied to those things that are not known. And this has always been the case. Even in biblical times, when miracles (it seems) were not uncommon, Paul wrote after having had a miraculous vision that "we see in a mirror dimly" (1 Cor. 13:12). The disciples, who walked with Jesus daily, had to have faith that Jesus was what he claimed to be, just as we must, for it could not be demonstrated. As Christians we believe because we do not know. We are not necessarily anti-intellectual; we just sense a realm of existence that cannot be known through demonstration.

I guess I should have realized that faith is blind and not let the comment bother me. Whether or not God exists cannot be known. If someone should attack your Christianity with the concept of blind faith or if it should ever assail you on its own, remember that that is simply the nature of belief. And, in terms of actual knowledge of the existence or non-existence of God, atheism, too, is blind.

Bradley Siebert is in a master's program in English at the University of Arizona in Tucson.

32. Quarterback Dilemma

Philippians 3:1-4

I get excited about college football with its teamwork, action, dedication, and sweat. Imagine a September afternoon at the stadium. On the first play from scrimmage the center snaps the ball to the quarterback. The ends run a deep pattern and one player gets open inside the ten. But now look at the quarterback. He's running the wrong direction with the ball. He's holding it high over his head shouting, "Look guys, I've got the football. Look Mom, this is a real college football game and I've got the ball!"

You and I know that's not the purpose for which the coach had that quarterback in the game. A quarterback is to use his access to the football to guide his team down the field and ultimately to score and win the game. It's that first down and the final score that determines whether the play has been successful. The quarterback who claims to be a success because he touched the ball deserves to be benched.

How will the coach straighten out his goofed-up player? Several things have to be made clear. First, he will indicate where the goal is. Having the ball, and running the wrong way damages the team's position. Second, he will emphasize that this is a team effort. There's a whole crew that's working together, and the whole team is affected by each person's action. Third, he will clarify the purpose of having a football in the game. Just touching the football isn't the point. On the other hand, you can't play the game without the ball.

In Philippians 3, Paul talks about making sure we're headed for the right goal. Verses 4, 5, and 6 represent Paul holding the football. Then in verses 7 through 11 he clarifies the goal he's working toward. He says that unless the things in the first list lead to knowing Christ, then it's like running the wrong way in the game. He can brag about his geneology and academic and professional accomplishments, but they are useless if they don't lead to knowing Christ. Bragging about his accomplishments is like saying, "I'm great, I got to touch the ball, " or running for the wrong goal.

I'm working hard toward the goal of a college degree. When graduation finally gets here, I'll be proud. I hope my family can join me for the day. It's sobering, though, to realize that my education is like a football. I can wave it around to impress people. I can use it to prove my points. Or, I can get down to work, using what I've got to help move the team toward the goal. In Paul's words, unless it leads to knowing Christ, it's all rubbish.

Nate Yoder is a senior history, English, secondary education major at Western Kentucky University at Bowling Green, Kentucky.

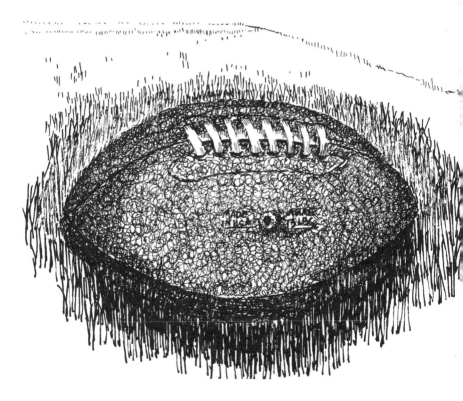

33. Patience

Consider it all joy, my brethren, when you meet various trials, for you know the testing of your faith produces steadfastness. And let steadfastness have its full effect, that you may be perfect and complete, lacking in nothing.
James 1:2-4

Patience is one of the fruits of the Spirit that is a challenge for many. To have the endurance to wait for God's will to happen is difficult and requires Christians to trust Christ completely.

In college many pressing matters appear to us. Often we feel that there is not time to consult God about them and we take them into our own hands. This is where trouble creeps in. Soon we discover that the hustle and bustle of college life has taken control of our lives. When we push the Lord's control into the back corner and become the controlling factor of our actions, failure will soon follow.

God is not satisfied with being tucked away to be pulled out only in times of trouble. God wants to guide our entire lives and direct us in our decisions. God does not promise that we will never face hardships once we become Christians. He says that we will face trials and temptations, but reassures us that he will be there to help us through them. In 1 Corinthians 10:13 Paul writes, "No temptation has overtaken you that is not common to man. God is faithful, and he will not let you be tempted beyond your strength, but with the temptation will also provide the way of escape, that you may be able to endure it." Through temptations God will make us stronger. We will develop patience that will result in total trust in God's decisions. With this trust and understanding, we as Christians will lack nothing.

What a wonderful promise! By enduring trials that test our faith, we will develop patience. With patience God promises that we will lack nothing. By listening to God we will find complete satisfaction.

Christians need to live each day to the fullest and not worry about what is to come in the future. Being patient means that we trust God's directions and believe that he will put all things together for his purpose. He promises us this in Romans 8:28: "We know that in everything God works for good with those who love him, and who are called according to his purpose."

Patience allows us to trust God for guidance in our lives. Patience is a virtue that takes time and constant work, but when it has been acquired it leaves one feeling content and secure.

Dear Lord, thank you for granting me security by teaching me patience. Next time temptations and trials face me, help me to lean on you and trust your guidance. Through these experiences I know that you will fulfill each of my needs according to your purpose. Thank you for your love and caring. Thanks for being in control of my life, especially when things here want to take control over me, and I am tempted to fall away. I just want to thank you for being here and taking me by the hand to guide me through my life. Amen.

Joyce Duerksen is a 1983 graduate of the University of Nebraska in Lincoln. She majored in home economics education.

34. Reflections on Psalm 71
(from a collection of nine poems)

*III. Thou who hast made me see many sore troubles wilt revive me
again. Psalm 71:20*

Her soul was a smooth stream stone
Gently floating, falling through the lime water,
Coming to rest and lie still on the clay-bottom
On the soft brown silt which cannot be felt
Peaceful, oh so peaceful.
   The flow cradled the stone
   Wiping, washing with cool specks of mud
   Back and forth, back and forth
   Gurgling a secret lullaby...shh
   Peaceful, oh so peaceful.
With rain came floods
And swift torrents rushed in upon the brook,
Altering, moving, changing its course
So that the stone was overturned
Unprotected and alone.
   Sprawled on dry land the stone succumbed
   To hot blasts from the sun;
   Birds pecked and scratched its mud-caked veneer,
   A soul of weakness and so hard—
   Unprotected and alone.

*VI. . . . from the depths of the earth thou wilt bring me up again. Thou
wilt increase my honor. . . . Psalm 71:20, 21*

As the young man fell
   he heard the curse of the crowd,
   the laugh of the opponent,
   the sob of his mouth.

   He felt the grit on his knee,
   the twist of his finger,
   the mud on his face.

   He saw the ball roll away,
   the fans leave the stands,
   the victory lost forever.

Another man fell,
  and he too heard the curse of the crowd,
  the laugh of the opponent,
  the sob of his mouth.

  He felt the grit on his knee,
  the twist of his finger
  the mud on his face.

  He saw the blood run down,
  the fans leave the hill,
  the victory won forever.

VII. My lips will shout for joy, when I sing praises to thee. . . . Psalm 71:23

  On that day
  O yes, that day!
  The air so crisp, and yet not cold
  we'll stand close and sing.

  Our notes, like silver frosted leaves
  will dance about our sides.
  Blown on the wind of love
  they weave
  and ring when tips collide.

Donna A. McAllister is a 1983 graduate of Eastern Mennonite College in Harrisonburg, Virginia. She majored in Bible and Christian ministries.

Terry Stutzman's home congregation is the Mennonite Church of Normal (Illinois). She studied at both Goshen and Bluffton colleges and graduated from Bluffton in 1982 with majors in English and art.

While a college student she wrote and illustrated for the campus newspapers. Terry currently serves as assistant director of Information Services at Goshen College.